"I've read your book and I really [e]njoyed the book. It was just what I neede[d]... [practical] approach. So refreshing to read [... to] succeed. The practical exercises in the book are very good and got me thinking about where I was going wrong and, crucially, what steps I need to take to improve my sales results. I read the book during a train journey and it really got me thinking about how I sell my services and myself to my clients."

- Lisa Scully-O'Grady, Ireland, www.tbms.ie

"I've just finished reading through Selling with Heart and I really really enjoyed it! I particularly liked the introductory background to you and what you have gone through as a sales woman. The language you have written in is so simple and easy to understand that I think you do a good job of 'humanising' the whole thing - it does not look so bad after all! And really, its just about being passionate, loving what you do and then applying methods that you highlight, methods that work.

It seems much more doable after that read. The content is so good I'll be referring back to it to make sure I stay on track. The advice and action points contained within were priceless. Your authenticity really came through and I like that. You come across real, passionate and wanting to keep things simple for the success of others."

- Sara Brown, UK, www.sarabrown.co.uk

"I have just finished reading your book. I found it concise in the various points and would assist anyone in helping them to become a Savvy Saleswoman/person. There were times during the book where I thought I knew everything you were going to say but I have learnt a few new things!!"

- Jo Stewart, UK, www.fivelakes.co.uk

"Selling with Heart is a very thoughtful, practical and insightful read. It is also considerately broken down into manageable portions with each section finishing in a convenient place to pause. I found the Perfect Elevator Pitch useful and was very interested in Choosing the Right Words which highlighted the benefits of modelling your spec to your target audience - an obvious choice but not done in the obvious way... I enjoyed reading the comments made by others which were included in the book, allowing me to look at issues through a different set of eyes. In summary - Selling with Heart - how to be 'Savvy' without being Pushy – like it."

- Joanna Clarke, UK, www.justforyou2.co.uk

"I am writing to give you some feedback. I love it! I loved the bit on intuition – this was so useful to me. It reminded me to listen to it! I love the way the last step ends in such an upbeat 'pep-talk' way. Really boosting that feeling of who you are and what you can do. For someone who 'just wants to be herself' this really resonates with me.

It's been really useful. I feel totally differently about 'sales'. Really it's just about being me, loving what I do and telling others about it – if they're interested in what I'm offering and who I am, they'll hire me and we'll work well together. If not, that's okay! Well, yes there's more to it, but that's in essence how I now feel about 'selling myself' and my work. Just need to practice all you've outlined – including my elevator speech."

- Claire Gillen, UK, www.create-a-life-you-love.com

Selling with Heart

Selling the Feminine Way

by Julie Roman

Copyright © 2009 Julie Roman

ISBN: 978-1-60910-013-1

All rights reserved. No part of this publication may be reproduced, stored in a retrieval system or transmitted in any form or by any means, including photocopying, electronic, mechanical, recording or otherwise, without the prior written permission of the author.

The information contained in this book is intended to provide helpful and informative material on the subject addressed. It is not intended to serve as a substitute for professional advice. Any use of the information in this book is at the reader's discretion. The author specifically disclaims any and all liability arising directly or indirectly from the use or application of any information contained in this book.

The individuals and websites referred to in the text are examples of what the author considers to be effective at the subject addressed. They are not an endorsement of any product or service.

Every effort has been made to identify and acknowledge the sources of the material quoted throughout the book. The author apologises for any errors or omissions and would be grateful to be notified of any corrections that should appear in any reprint or new edition.

BookLocker.com, Inc.
2009

Acknowledgements

I'd like to thank my husband for helping me to put this book together and for his support. To Sam who edited the original draft. To the women who contributed their stories about using their intuition. To my family who have always believed in me. To my friends who have encouraged my business dreams, listened to my many ideas over the years, and who have lifted me up when I have been down! I also want to thank bestselling author and visionary Nick Williams who has inspired me to dream big and follow my heart. His invaluable guidance made this book happen.

About the Author

I wasn't always a **Savvy Saleswoman**! Prior to getting a sales job, I'd worked for 10 years in admin roles. I struggled with the traditional way of selling. I also didn't like the hard sell approach. It just didn't 'feel right' to me and I felt my clients deserved a lot better. I worked hard and achieved my sales targets but was by no means a high flyer.

I always strive to be successful in everything I do. So I decided to reflect on the way I was selling; so that I could change my approach to getting sales. I consolidated my thoughts into five simple steps. By focusing on these five steps I found that my commission and earnings levels were rising dramatically.

Using these five steps made me VERY SUCCESSFUL!

Within a short space of time I went from nowhere in the league tables to the top saleswoman in the region. I was making sales with less effort and earning more money. I'd discovered Selling the Feminine Way, the secret that turned my sales skills around that I call Selling with Heart. I now run **Savvy Saleswoman** supporting women who want help to do the same.

Do you believe in your product and love what you do? Selling with Heart has helped me grow from an administrator with no sales skills into a **Savvy Saleswoman**. If you follow the simple steps it can do the same for you.

Julie Roman
September 2009

Author's Note

The stories in this book are true; however names have been changed to protect privacy.

Contents

Welcome 1

Step 1: Preparation 7
   Know your products and services inside and out 7
   Acquiring new clients 9
   Attracting the clients who value what you do 10
   So, what do you do? 10
   I'm not a sales coach 13
   Are you an expert? 14
   Raising your profile 16
   Making sales appointments 17
   Why it's good practice to reconfirm the meeting 18
   Do your homework on your potential clients 19
   Build up a picture of the person you will be meeting ..19
   Fear of saying the wrong thing 19
   First impressions really do count! 20
   Knowledge is power 22
   Summary 23
   Review 24

Step 2: Communication 25
   Revealing who you are 26
   Being authentic in sales 27
   Selling in a way you feel ok about 28
   Using your own words 28
   Speaking from the heart 30
   Being a good listener 30
   Choosing the right words 31
   Questions to aid communication 33
   Visual clues 34
   How to tell if you are connecting 35
   Summary 37
   Review 38

Step 3: Intuition 39
It's your time to shine! 40
So what is intuition? 40
Valuing your intuition 41
How do you use intuition in business? 41
Your intuitive signals 42
Making your intuitive signals stronger 49
Summary 51
Review 52

Step 4: Facilitation 53
Example: Kay Parsons - Life Coaching Taster Session 55
Example: Jane Lewis - Web Design Sales Meeting 57
Match products and services 59
Focus on the outcomes 59
Overcome the block 60
Reveal who you are 60
Talk money 61
Summarise what you've discussed 63
Have faith! 63
Treat your clients respectfully 64
Manage expectations 64
Once you've made the sale 65
Summary 68
Review 69

Step 5: Reflection 71
Two selling truths 72
Negotiating on price 72
Getting your pricing right 73
Knowing the minimum amount you can charge 74
How many weeks do you work per year? 74
Feeling undervalued by your clients 75
Using your site to let people know what you charge 76
Asking clients about the budget they have available 76
Making sure you are talking to the right people 77
Staying focused on selling 77
Keeping sales records 78

Allowing for the quiet times 79
Keeping all the balls in the air 79
Don't spend all your time doing what you love! 80
Trusting your heart and believing you'll do well 81
Savvy sales idea: Bread and Butter 82
Savvy sales idea: Consider Selling InfoProducts 84
Overcoming fears 85
Affirmations 85
Acceptance 86
Visualisations 87
Energy 90
Gratitude 90
Summary 91
Review 92
Last thoughts 93
Thank you! I'd love to hear from you 93

Welcome

Many women want to make more money but struggle with the idea of 'selling' to do this. We know how great our products and services are but we avoid selling them (and ourselves). We don't tell enough people about what we can do for them. This means that we don't get enough clients to buy from us and so our cash flow varies from month to month.

We also fail to fully maximise the potential of selling our expertise. We can often over deliver and under charge. We aren't clear in our minds about the real value of what we do. This means that we let people negotiate us down to a price that we can't really afford to do the work for, and when we cost out our true hourly rate we aren't earning what we're really worth.

The hard sell doesn't feel right to us. We've all experienced the hard sell at some point in our lives and don't want to act like that. We don't want to manipulate people into buying from us, or to come across as being pushy. We want to treat our clients with respect.

We lose sight of the money making activities. We fill our day with anything else that we enjoy doing. We tell ourselves that we are too busy with these other things and that we need to put off the sales activities until another day. We don't have any systems in place to ensure that we stay focused on meeting our sales goals.

Often we feel inspired to leave the corporate world to start businesses in areas that we feel passionate about. We want to stay true ourselves; so that we can be successful without losing who we are. We don't want to use a sales technique that means we have to sacrifice our values or ethics. We want a 21$^{st.}$ Century sales solution that honours the authentic way we do business today.

This book tackles these issues and much more. Selling with Heart introduces you to an effective alternative - *Selling the Feminine Way*. It aims to give you all the practical information you need to be successful selling your products and services without selling out yourself or your clients. At the end of the book, I share a few last thoughts and suggestions on ways you can take this further.

To begin on your journey today, first look at your own experience of what selling means to you.

Try this:

- Ask yourself: How do I feel about selling?
- Why is this view of selling holding me back?
- What's stopped me from turning this around?
- What goals will being able to sell help me to achieve?

Notes:

When we think about a bad sales experience what pops into most people's heads is car, insurance, door to door or telesales people. It invokes feelings of being pressured into something we don't want, haggling over the price and the salesperson not taking the time or interest to find out what we want.

This book aims to show you that there is another way.

Try this:

- Reflect for a moment on a bad sales experience.
- Now reflect on a good sales experience. (This can either be you selling something or being sold to).
- Now consider what the key differences are between the experiences and note them down.

Notes:

Consider where you are now and where you want to be. As you read, make notes on how you will put the ideas into action.

Try this:

- Ask yourself: What am I doing now? *For example: I get really nervous when talking in front of a potential client and I don't feel that I'm enthusiastic enough about my products and services.*
- What action can I take as a result of reading this book? *I must prepare more and do background research about the client. I need to reveal more of who I am and list 6 ways my service will benefit the client.*
- Where do I want to be? *To talk confidently about the service I provide. To overcome my fears that make me avoid selling. To be able to sell in a way I feel ok about.*

Notes:

So let's get started!

Step 1: Preparation

Selling with Heart teaches you how to be well prepared so that you have: all the facts about your products and services at your fingertips, the right paperwork to hand to get the sale completed and the invoice paid quickly, a qualified appointment which means that the person is fully briefed on the purpose of the meeting, you have done your homework on the person you will be meeting and the meeting has been re-confirmed so that you don't waste any of your valuable time.

Know your products and services inside and out

You need to know everything about your products and services; so that you can answer your clients' questions with confidence. To buy from you, your clients will want to know how your products and services will enhance their lives. So be clear in your mind about the **benefits** of what you do.

Benefits are subjective. For example: One person may like having a mobile phone for emergencies, which means that if her car breaks down she can ring a breakdown service. Another may like having a mobile phone for business, which means that his clients can contact him when he is out of the office.

If your products and services are aimed at a certain group of people you can list the benefits based on what you know will appeal to the group. This is a really useful exercise for writing marketing material and content for your website. If you don't know for sure you can always ask your clients what they are!

Try this:

- Ask yourself: What will my clients be able to do after buying from me that they couldn't do before?
- List all of these benefits.

Notes:

You also need to prove that buying the product or service will be a good decision. You want to tell your clients about what they'll be getting for their money. These are the **features** of the product or service. Each feature is a fact about the product that will offer a personal benefit to the buyer.

Features are facts. For example: One person may like the fact that a particular dishwasher has a time delay, which means that he can take advantage of cheaper electricity. Another will like the fact that the design is compact, which means that it will fit into the space she has in her kitchen.

Try this:

- Ask yourself: What facts will your clients want to know about your products?
- List all of these features.

Notes:

In Step 4: Facilitation, you will discover how to identify the personal benefits that your buyers are looking for. Once you are aware of these, you can then match the products or services that will best meet their needs.

Acquiring new clients

Your goal is to get your business known by the people who need what you do. You want to generate enquiries to get a steady flow of potential clients to your door as efficiently and cost effectively as possible. Once you've got them in front of you (or your website) you need them to buy from you.

The more it costs you to generate the enquiry measured against how much money the client spends on your products and services over a period of time is what gives you your Return on Investment (ROI) calculation. You obviously want to make a profit and so you don't want to spend more on acquiring clients than you receive in income from them. One cost-effective way of acquiring new clients is through word of mouth marketing. I also use the following visualisation technique to help me attract the clients I love to work with.

Attracting the clients who value what you do

By picturing what you want and believing 100% that you can have it, you can begin to attract what you want into your life. In your journal, write down all the qualities that your ideal client possesses. Then lie down or sit comfortably. Close your eyes and visualise yourself as being magnetic to all of the people who you'd like to be your clients. (There is more on visualisation in Step 5: Reflection). You can also say this affirmation to yourself:

- I attract clients I love to work with.

So, what do you do?

I hate the thought of coming across as 'pushy' when people ask me "so, what do you do?" This section looks at the solutions I have discovered that may help you overcome this problem; so that you can answer this question confidently and with ease.

Have you ever struggled to describe what you do? It is a real waste of an opportunity when you walk away from someone who could either have turned into a client, or referred you to people looking for the solutions you provide. So, to overcome this in the future you need to create your own perfect (elevator) pitch.

For your perfect pitch to be really effective it needs to be simple, short and snappy. Try not to waffle. Practice it until you are comfortable with what you are saying and it doesn't sound as if you are reading from a script.

The perfect pitch gives people a powerful introduction to what you do. Taking less than 30 seconds (the time you'd have travelling in an elevator) to capture people's attention.

Once you've created your perfect pitch you can use it to market your products and services face to face and to spread the word effectively about what you do.

Try this:

Create your own perfect pitch. Here are some ideas you may like to include.

- The life changing event that gave birth to your business.
- The problem you discovered you had the solution for.
- Why you are so passionate about what you do.
- Why you are qualified to fill the space in your niche.
- The results you have achieved for yourself and your clients.

Notes:

I'm not a sales coach

I like the "three-second statement" that John Purkiss (http://twitter.com/JohnPurkiss) and David Royston-Lee describe in their gem of a book Brand You (www.brandyou.info) (ISBN: 0955116422). This means that when you are asked, "so what do you do?" That you give people a description that is more than just, "I'm a life coach", which can lead to little interest from the other person and can stop the conversation flat! John and David advise that you should make this first impression memorable:

"*Your three-second statement helps to communicate your unique combination and makes people remember you.*"

As I was reading this section, it made me think about the times I've been to a party and the host has introduced me to someone new. The great hosts give you interesting facts about the person, "This is Emma Smith; she's an artist and a keen horse rider." This brief, but expressive, introduction makes it easier for you to engage in conversation.

I completed the exercise in the book and created this statement: "*I'm Julie Roman, a Selling with Heart coach.* Most of my clients are women." I didn't want to just say that I am a sales coach. So, I chose these particular words because *Selling with Heart* is new to most people and I can then tell them about it. They may also wonder why I mainly coach women; so I can explain my reasons for this too. I'll see how I get on with this statement, I'm sure it will need some tweaking!

If it works, it will lead me nicely into the perfect pitch that succinctly describes what I do. But don't get me wrong, I'm not doing this to manipulate people. I'm just being prepared as I don't want to waste an opportunity to help more people who may be struggling with the problems I can solve.

Your aim is to be able to talk fluently about what you can do for people. If it isn't right for the people you are talking to, they may like what you do anyway and feel compelled to refer you to the people they know, who are more suitable.

Are you an expert?

We all have something special to offer. We all have different life experiences and journeys that have brought us to varied destinations. People are willing to pay for your expertise because they want to know what you know. We all crave the solutions to our problems. That's why we spend millions on self-help books, seminars and courses delivered by people who have proven that they hold the answers that we seek. They may have been recommended to us by friends and family. We may have read a book, or been given a taster of what they can do for us and we like what we see and hear.

Try this:

Think about an expert you trust.

- How did you first get introduced to this expert?
- What made you trust this expert?
- What results did the expert help you achieve?
- What products have you bought from this expert?
- Why would you recommend this expert to your friends and family?

Notes:

You may find that the person become an expert through sharing her life experience publicly. The expert may have very few academic qualifications. You may have even read reviews on websites where people haven't liked the advice given by the expert.

Being an expert means standing tall in your shoes because you know in your heart that what you do can enhance other people's lives. That your life experience can be used positively to light the way for other people in similar circumstances. That the solutions only you yourself can provide to others are valuable. This can be measured by the people you can help as your service is valuable to them.

Raising your profile

Become known as an expert by writing articles and ask high quality websites to add them to their content. This can help to build your credibility and your search engine ranking if you ask for a link back to your website. This is a win-win as it gives people a taster of what you do and also raises your profile.

Once you are comfortable that you are an expert you may even attract offers from magazines, newspapers, or radio looking for you to share what you know. In return for your contribution you can ask for a mention of your business and get your contact details printed, such as your website address and phone number.

Each time you get approached to give a talk, or write an article it may mean stepping out of your comfort zone for a while, but in my experience, each time it gets a little easier. There is also nothing more rewarding than getting some correspondence from someone who you have made a difference to. You also never know what new doors will open for you. A few years ago, I was approached for some very lucrative consultancy work because I was a resident expert on a high profile site for women in business.

I know it can be hard to view yourself as an expert. Taking a higher profile can also open you up to criticism. We all have our fears that we struggle with (we will look at how to overcome self-limiting fears in Step 5: Reflection).

I started writing this book a couple of years ago and have only now felt that the timing was right for me to publish it. Lots of doors have opened for me since I trusted my intuition and made the decision to create **Savvy Saleswoman**. I think that sometimes it's a matter of timing and being ready for all the positives and negatives that being seen as an expert can bring.

Making sales appointments

There is nothing more annoying than spending hours travelling to a meeting to find that it has been a total waste of your time! When making a new appointment over the telephone find out as much as you can about what they are looking for and the price they are prepared to pay. This helps you to discover whether you will be able to meet their expectations of what you can actually do for them.

I hate cold calling and so I always make new appointments from networking, via article marketing, social networking and my website. My best practice is to try to contact the person promptly if they have left an enquiry via a website or answer phone.

Explain as much as you can about what you do, including what the meeting entails, how long it should last and what they need to bring if the meeting is face to face. After the call, send an email or letter with the date, time and meeting place and then reconfirm the day before to ensure that the potential client is still able to make it.

Why it's good practice to reconfirm the meeting

I learned this the hard way! When I was a rookie salesperson I'd already had one sales meeting with the potential client and had arranged a second (evening) appointment to complete the paperwork for the products that we'd agreed that the guy needed.

In between the first and second appointments my sales manager asked me when I next had a second appointment booked in as he needed to sit in on one to assess me. So we arranged for him to sit in on this evening appointment.

Now my sales manager hated doing evening appointments but said he would come along anyway. We arrived at the house and knocked on the door. The guy was still living with his parents.

His mum ushered us into their front room and made us a cup of tea. We waited and waited and his mum said that he'd give her son a call. I hadn't reconfirmed the appointment and he told her he was sorry and that he'd totally forgotten about it!

As she explained this to us, I felt so embarrassed that I'd not followed it up. My sales manager was fuming and I just wanted to dig a hole and get into it. So I've always reconfirmed appointments from that date forward!

Do your homework on your potential clients

Before you meet with potential clients, try to find out as much as you can about them (and their company if applicable). This gives you a sense of the organisation and an insight into the people behind the business. You can look for clues such as:

- What impression does the website give me?
- Is there an 'about us' section and details of the person/people you will be meeting?
- What attitude does the website and marketing material convey?
- Where is the business located (home office, business address etc.)?
- Do a search has the person published any articles, been interviewed, featured on any websites etc?

Build up a picture of the person you will be meeting

Try not to make too many assumptions about the person or the business, but stick to the facts that you gather and the overall impression that all of these clues are giving you. You can use this exercise to give you a foundation for the meeting as it will give you more of a personal impression about the business. It helps you with building rapport at the beginning of the meeting as you can ask people about the things they have done. It also shows that you have done your homework!

Fear of saying the wrong thing

It's a good confidence builder to do a mental rehearsal but don't go over too much in your mind before you meet with your client as the conversation may then sound scripted rather than natural. I catch myself mentally having a conversation with the client as I am on my way to an appointment, or waiting for the client to arrive, and have to tell myself to STOP and think about something else so that I don't start worrying about what I'm going to say!

Instead, do your homework and know everything you can about the client, what they are looking for and how your products or services work. This is so that you can let your practical sales skills and intuition kick in (more on this in Step 3) without trying to control what you are saying by sticking to a pre-prepared script.

You will be more open so you can sense how to keep the conversation flowing. You can react to what is being said and control the direction that the conversation is going in. Otherwise you will be more focused on the words you are saying and you won't be truly listening and modifying what you are saying to suit the needs of the potential client.

First impressions really do count!

How do you want people to see you?

- Dress code – getting it right for your business.
- Professionalism – being good at time keeping and delivering on your promises.
- Being organised – preparing materials such as: business cards, leaflets, brochures, presentations and order forms.

Dress code

It can feel great not to have to wear stuffy corporate attire, especially if your office is at home where you can work all day in your pyjamas if you want to! What I mean by 'getting it right for your business' is about fitting in with your client by mirroring their dress code.

For example, do they work outdoors? Do they work in an office? Will they be wearing a suit or more casual attire? You may prefer to dress somewhere in between casual and smart so that you don't make your clients feel out of place, but still give a professional first impression.

Professionalism

If you look at websites and marketing material in your area of expertise you will most likely find that the standard of professionalism varies. Calling people back when you say you will. Contacting email enquiries promptly. Paying invoices on time. Delivering what you say you can (or explaining within good time why you can't).

These all encompass the art of good customer service, which seems to be sadly lacking in the business world today. People appreciate quality; they value it and are prepared to pay for it. It makes good business sense to work this way and to always work hard to maintain a consistent level of professionalism.

Being organised

This pays dividends in the long run. Create your invoices and order forms ready for when you make your first sale. You want to keep the momentum going when you've made a sale. You can buy legal documents to help you with this online. There are lots of companies who offer this service if you do a search on the internet. My bank helped me to create a standing order form.

I also spent time when I set up my company creating spreadsheets to keep tabs on my invoice payments and sales records (more on keeping sales records in Step 5). You can also create other documents easily in word:

- Quotation
- Proposal form
- Welcome letter
- What happens next letter
- Standing order form

You can then either print off what you need and take it with you to the meeting, or fill in what you need to and email or post it as soon as you've got back to your office. The meeting is still fresh in your client's mind and it is one less thing to add to your to do list. It also demonstrates that you are efficient and can act quickly to get things done for your clients.

Knowledge is power

Prepare as much as you can before the meeting and then relax and feel confident. Don't underestimate how much you know about what you do! But, if you don't know something tell them you'll find out and get back to them as soon as you can after the meeting.

Summary

- Focus on the benefits when thinking about the points you want to make in the sales meeting (the results that the person will achieve from buying your products or services) as this is what people want to know before they will buy.

- Know the features so that you can tell your clients about what they'll be getting for their money.

- Practice your own elevator pitch so that you can confidently tell potential clients about what you do.

- Get everything ready before the sales meeting so that you can complete any paperwork whilst the person is in the mindset that they are ready to buy.

Review

Congratulations! You have now completed the first step of the sales book. Take some time to complete these simple exercises to help you review Preparation:

- Which areas of Step 1 do you feel are causing you the most problems?
- What action do you want to take to overcome these problems?
- What timeframe do you want to give yourself to complete this action?

Notes:

Step 2: Communication

The word 'sales' can often fill people with terror, yet it is the traditional concept of selling that most people associate with. However, we are all salespeople – we sell a holiday location to our partners, we sell ourselves at an interview, we sell the concept of outdoor play to our children because we know it's good for them. We do all this without losing ourselves or exaggeration – it's simply an extension of who we are.

Your products and services have been created by you and so are unique (as you are). You may have discovered you had the solution to a problem, or experienced a life changing event that gave birth to your business. You can use your own life experiences to illustrate the points that you are making during the sales meeting.

You can share stories and your personality to make people feel more connected to you. We are naturally attracted to the energy of the people who are truly passionate about what they do. You can be yourself and make selling simply an extension of who you are!

Being yourself in sales also means that you can attract more people who are like you as new clients. We tend to mix with people who are easy to get on with, and mirror ourselves in some way. You may find that the clients who contact you share the same personality traits, or have the same outlook on life, or the same work ethic as you.

It can be really enjoyable working with clients who have similar standards and way of looking at life as you. These people are more open to seeing the value in what you do. Word soon spreads amongst their friends and family when you do a good job for them.

Revealing who you are

When you are working for yourself you don't need to put up barriers like you did in the corporate world. You can be more at ease and afford to take more risks in opening up to your clients. You don't necessarily have to make out that your business is larger than it is, or hide that you work from home, or work alone. You can be authentic and reveal who you are. I'd like to ask you to do three things today:

1. Spend some time thinking about what would stop you being yourself in sales.
2. Ask yourself: Does the thought of revealing more about who you are in a sales meeting scare you?
3. What is this fear based on?

Notes:

In corporate life we get in the habit of wearing a mask to hide who we really are inside. We try to fit in with our peers and to conform to the way things are done by the organisations we work for. You can choose to take off this mask and reveal the real you.

We all hate the cheesy salesperson that comes across as fake. By being yourself, you are treating people with respect, showing that you empathise with their problems and you are using a sales technique that is simply an extension of who you are.

You come across to potential clients as honest and natural. You build stronger relationships, which in turn helps you to:

- Attract more clients
- Boost repeat sales
- Receive referrals

Being authentic in sales

I tendered for a large project and went up against two big web design consultancies. One of these had offices in London and New York. (I was working from a computer workstation in my bedroom at the time!) I used my intuition to guide me at the sales meeting and acted on any intuitive signals I received.

However, I thought that I had blown my chances as I had revealed who I was. I felt it was right to let them know that I had set up on my own and that I didn't employ staff, that I mainly outsource work to other women in business. They liked the fact that I wasn't a large business and that I could focus solely on each client's projects (as I only work with a handful of clients at a time) and I was awarded the work.

Being authentic means trusting yourself and being true to you. Opening up and allowing who you really are to shine through. Tapping into the power of your own intuition and letting it guide you. We will look at intuition in Step 3.

Selling in a way you feel ok about

I do recognise that there is a hard sell approach that works for some people. I've worked in sales teams where every single person has had their own unique sales style, which has worked well for them. Some of the methods they used would feel alien to me. So I only use a sales style that I feel ok about and that is aligned with my values.

I would encourage you to discover your own sales style. Be totally comfortable with what you are saying and choose your words carefully so that you stay true to yourself. Selling with Heart means that you sell in a way you feel ok about. It is an extension of who you are, rather than feeling you have to sell out, or lose yourself to be successful in sales.

When you choose to make a sale this way you are genuinely providing something of value, are honest about what you can do and you offer your product or service at a fair price. This is the reason that people will buy from you. You've no need to use sales techniques to manipulate people and 'talk them into it'.

Using your own words

Being able to communicate effectively is an essential element of Selling with Heart. This means developing a connection so that you can sense whether the products or services you are offering are right for your clients, then (and only then) will you recommend them.

I was recently buying car insurance over the phone and the salesman was running through a script. I wanted to put my husband on the policy and he noticed from my husband's date of birth that his birthday was only a few weeks away. I am paraphrasing but this is along the lines of what the guy said to me:

"It's your husband's birthday in a couple of weeks, what are you buying him?"

It had been quite a tedious conversation to that point and I brightened up and thought great he's taking some interest in me. So I said,

"Oh we're going to a concert."

At which point I thought he'd ask me who we were seeing to build a bit of rapport. But no – instead he said:

"Have you thought of buying him some car insurance for his birthday?"

He then carried on with his script and I was left speechless! (And he didn't get the sale!)

You need to be able to build rapport and one of the easiest ways to do this is to take a real interest in the person you are speaking to. You can use your intuition (which we'll look at in Step 3) combined with the following communication techniques to ensure you are connecting:

- Speaking from the heart
- Being a good listener
- Choosing the right words
- Questions to aid communication
- How to tell if you are connecting
- Visual clues

Speaking from the heart

You know when you are speaking from the heart as you feel good. The other person is responding positively to what you are saying and the sales meeting is going well. You and the other person leave the meeting feeling energised. When you aren't speaking from the heart, the reverse can be true. You may both be having a bad time. You may feel deflated after the meeting has ended.

Speaking from the heart is all about taking the time to listen and to check whether people are ready to hear what you have to say and only communicating in a way that will empower others. You can sense if something doesn't feel right to you. This can tell you whether you, and the words you are choosing, are connecting. This can also tell you if you are both getting the most from your time together.

Being a good listener

If we are honest, how many of us really listen? Don't we prefer the friends we have that are good listeners? We feel more valued when we feel we've been listened to. Developing a connection is all about being a good listener and giving people the opportunity to really be heard.

Be totally present with the person throughout the meeting or sales call; this is the only way that you can really get to connect with them. You need to clear your mind and switch off what's going on in your life. Focus on the person and maintain good eye contact with them.

Choosing the right words

Have you ever attended a training course and been asked to complete a questionnaire to find out how you like to learn? I discovered that I was a visual learner. Recently, I was having a conversation with a guy and he took out a piece of paper and started drawing diagrams to illustrate the points he was making. At the time it helped me to understand what he was saying and I can still visualise the drawings, which helps me to remember what he was communicating to me.

We tend to interpret information in different ways. We aren't consciously aware of our senses but we constantly access them to process and make sense of information. I learned about the following when reading 'The Life Coaching Handbook by Curly Martin' (ISBN: 1899836713). I'm not a NLP Practitioner but found this really interesting and so did a bit more research on the internet and this is my understanding of how it works.

The three senses **Auditory** (sounds), **Visual** (images) and **Kinaesthetic** (touch and internal feelings) are referred to in Neuro Linguistic Programming as Representational Systems. We have only one preferred representational system. You can identify this through people's speech patterns. These can then help you with choosing the right words in your sales meetings.

For example, if you are speaking to a 'Visual' person they can use terms such as:

- See
- Look
- Picture
- View
- Show

An 'Auditory' person can use terms such as:

- Listen
- Hear
- Sounds
- Question
- Tell

A 'Kinaesthetic' person can use terms such as:

- Feel
- Touch
- Hold
- Grasp
- Catch on

When you are getting to know the client at the beginning of the meeting, or sales call, you can listen out for clues that can tell you the person's preferred representational system e.g.:

- Auditory - "That sounds good to me, or I hear what you are saying."
- Visual - "I can see how it may look that way, or I can't quite picture it."
- Kinaesthetic - "I don't completely grasp the concept, or "I think it will catch on."

So, in my example, if the guy had discovered early on that I was a 'Visual' person he could have used terms such as: see, look, picture, view, show, as well as his diagrams to communicate more effectively with me.

Questions to aid communication

Using revealing questions helps your clients to communicate the problems and issues that they face. There are three types of revealing questions:

1. Open questions start with:
   - What
   - When
   - Where
   - Why
   - Who
   - How

These are designed to get the client talking to you. To start the conversation you can ask an open question to discover what the client wants to get out of the meeting. You can simply ask:

What would you like to achieve from our meeting today?

The main thing to remember is to ask an open question and then be silent! Ask revealing questions that encourage your potential clients to tell you about the issues they are facing and what they are looking for. People will generally talk in terms of aims and goals they have for themselves and problems they need to solve. Make mental or written notes as you listen, so that you can probe deeper into a subject that they talk to you about.

2. Probing questions

- *Tell me ...*
- *I'm interested in learning more about...*

3. Closed questions

Closed questions can be useful in certain circumstances where you just need a simple yes or no answer. For example, to open up a connection at the start of the meeting you can use a closed question:

- *Is it ok if I ask you about...?*

Visual clues

You can also use visual clues to determine whether your words are connecting with the people you are speaking to face to face. These visual clues give you an indication of what is going on subconsciously in the other person. These non-verbal clues include:

Person is interested
- Good eye contact
- Hand to cheek (thinking about what you are saying)
- Tilted head
- Stroking chin
- Matching (their body direction is the same as yours)

Person is disinterested
- Bad eye contact such as looking away
- Folded arms
- Their body direction is facing away from yours
- Confused facial expression

Notice the difference to your communication when you match and mismatch body language. Matching body language involves sitting in a similar way to the other person, making the same amount of eye contact. Mirroring means the other person is a reflection of you. Body language in different cultures has different meanings. So you can check your interpretation of body language by also asking open questions to discover whether the person is getting the full meaning of what you are saying.

How to tell if you are connecting

The easiest way to tell if your words are connecting is by summarising your discussion, repeating back what you understand are the person's needs and what she wants from you. Your intuition can also tell you if your words are connecting. You may experience a fluttering feeling in your stomach. This can happen at various times throughout the conversation. You may feel a bit uneasy, which will go as soon as you move the conversation back on track.

Also be aware of any visual clues that can show you if your words are set at the right level and that the person is listening to and accepting what you are saying. If not, check for understanding and go over the points you are trying to make from a different angle (it may just be a case of you needing to simplify the language you are using).

If you feel uncomfortable and sense an energy shift in the other person or a change in their body language, check to see whether you've started introducing details about your products or have touched a nerve through something you've said. Simply say to them that you sense you have said something that has made them uncomfortable and then do what you can to put it right by using your senses to guide you.

Tone of voice is also important as you are effectively using your words to help a person to relax, begin trusting you and open up through your questioning, which is helping elicit sometimes personal information.

Summary

- Be yourself and make selling simply an extension of who you are.
- Speak from the heart by only communicating in a way that will empower others.
- Facilitate the meeting by using revealing questions. This will help people to open up and tell you about the problems that they need to solve.
- Focus 100% on the other person, maintain good eye contact and remember to listen attentively!
- During the meeting practice using body language to build rapport and improve communication.
- Be totally comfortable with what you are saying and choose your words carefully so that you stay true to yourself.

Review

Congratulations! You have now completed the second step of the sales book. Take some time to complete these simple exercises to help you review Communication:

- Which areas of Step 2 do you feel are causing you the most problems?
- What action do you want to take to overcome these problems?
- What timeframe do you want to give yourself to complete this action?

Notes:

Step 3: Intuition

The women that I speak to feel that they don't want to use hard sell techniques to manipulate people into buying from them. They also don't want to sell out and sacrifice their values and ethics in order to make a sale. They sell responsibly because they believe in what they do and know in their hearts that they are doing the right thing for their clients.

They know this because they use their intuition to sense their clients' emotions. This gives them an insight into any concerns that each client may have, which they can then address before the person makes a commitment to buy.

When we buy from someone, we weigh up whether we trust the person and whether the relationship will be right for us. This is because we don't want to feel that we are being conned, or that we will lose out in some way from a buying decision. So, we tend to buy from people we trust or on recommendation from someone we know.

When we picture sales people we often conjure up images of a certain stereotype using hard sell techniques to 'force' us into buying something. So it's no wonder that many women feel that they can't sell because they know they can't sell their products and services in that way.

Selling with Heart offers you an alternative way of selling that combines sales techniques with your intuition to sell responsibly i.e. to never push people into a sale. It harnesses the power of your intuition to help you to create a stronger, more rewarding connection with your clients.

In my experience, this overcomes the biggest barrier that people have – the fear of being conned – it helps people to feel that we have their best interests at heart. This often means that they come back to us when they need further advice and give referrals to people they know.

It's your time to shine!

Many of us are moving away from the corporate world and are starting businesses teaching others what we have learned through our own experiences. We believe in our product and love what we do. We can tap into our intuition to help us with this.

Many sales techniques were developed prior to this service orientated way of working. In my opinion, Selling with Heart suits people who want to work this way. Of course we need to make money, but we want to do so in a way that honours who we are. We want to be successful by staying true to ourselves.

We know how to help the people who have the problems we have experienced ourselves. We can offer the solutions that will help them to overcome their blocks and to attain their goals. I believe that we are connected in some way to the people we are here to help, and that our service is not only valuable to them, but can enhance our lives too.

So what is intuition?

Intuition is outside of our five senses and is often referred to as our *sixth sense*. It is an inner voice that guides us. Intuition is most commonly referred to as a 'gut feeling' or 'gut instinct'.

Listening to your intuition isn't always easy. It can mean changing your way of life, stepping out of your comfort zone and taking action based on your heart rather than your head.

If your intuition is buried so deep that you can hardly hear it whisper, you may not be able to make a decision confident in the knowledge that it is totally right for you. Sometimes in the beginning you have to weigh up all the options, listen to your intuition, then make the decision and let go of any attachment to the outcome.

Valuing your intuition

I've read quotes from business leaders who have talked about intuition. What I like about these high profile people is that they know the value of using their gut instinct in business and are happy to talk about it.

Generally, in corporate life, it is perfectly acceptable to speak about our intangible skills such as 'communication' and 'creativity'; however, I'm sure if you think about it, there will be very few occasions when your intuition was mentioned. For instance, can you remember a time when you were asked to make a decision at work based on your gut feeling?

How do you use intuition in business?

Once you've mastered the techniques that I'm going to show you on the following pages, you can tap into your intuition at any time when you need help not just with selling but also with evaluating your business choices. Sometimes you can look at all the facts laid out in front of you and get no clear indication of the way forward. This is the time to use your intuition to guide you in the right direction.

As intuition is a sixth sense it is linked into a bigger picture than you can currently see. So you may find that trusting your intuition takes you in a new direction than you were expecting. This can be uncomfortable at times as you may have to face obstacles that need to be cleared out of the way before you can start moving forward again.

Look again at a time in your life when you've made a decision that you can now see with hindsight opened up new opportunities later on. For instance, this can be when you had a gut feeling to take a particular job. You may have hated that job at the time, but looking back at it, you can see that you needed the experience for a better job that you took later on, or even for skills that it gave you for your business life.

Your intuitive signals

You can start listening to your own intuition by first becoming aware of your intuitive signals. These are how our intuition communicates with us and our intuitive signals are unique to each of us. Intuitive signals can be for example an 'inner nudge', a 'hunch', a 'repetitive thought' or a sensation that something simply doesn't 'feel right'.

These are some of the ways that intuitive signals make themselves known to the women who helped me with research for this book:

Laura said, "My body tells me to listen to my intuition by giving me the constant desire to scream if I don't do it. I get a lump in my throat when I am doing something contrary to my inner voice. When I recognize I am fighting against my intuition I feel almost physically sick because ultimately I know I have only myself to blame - and that's annoying!"

Margaret said, "When my intuition is guiding me I just feel something is trying to tell me something. It keeps going on in my head until I act or reason with the inner voice. I generally take notice because the message is usually right."

My own intuition usually guides me through repetitive thoughts and a feeling that if I follow it will guide me to new opportunities. I've always used it in selling as a wise guide that helps me to attract new sales opportunities. It also helps me during the sales meeting to sense whether I am connecting with the client. When I have trusted my gut feel to reveal more information about myself than I normally would, it has resulted in a sale.

Your intuitive signals will be distinctive to you and you may need to do some work to find out what they are. Use the following intuitive signals exercise to become clear about how your intuition communicates with you.

Try this:

- How does your body feel when your intuition is trying to tell you something?
- What thoughts/feelings/physical sensations can you remember?
- What was the result the last time you listened to your intuition?

Notes:

You can strengthen your intuitive signals by becoming more aware of each occurrence. To start with, you may wish to keep a record of any intuitive guidance you receive and a record of each time you act, or don't act, on its signals and what happens as a result.

All of the women that I asked to do the above exercise found it really hard! Intuition can be such an involuntary part of our decision making process that we aren't even aware of it. However, it can also be the case that we've stopped listening to our inner voice and so any intuitive signals we receive are so faint that we can hardly hear them whisper. So I would urge you to do the exercise and see what it tells you.

Try this:

Think about any times in your life where you didn't listen to your intuition and with hindsight you wish you had.

- What happened?

Notes:

I've had times in my life when I haven't listened to my intuition. When I let my intuition guide me I can't always see the outcome but I know the journey will be a wonderful one! It has led me to many experiences that I would have missed out on through fear, or simply not being in the right place at the right time.

Whenever I've gone against my gut feeling, or sought out advice and not trusted my intuition, I've always regretted it. However, these times were showing me that I wasn't completely ready to trust myself and my intuitive signals. I was looking for other people to make the decisions for me. I didn't have enough faith in myself and so was bypassing my own intuition.

If you find this happening to you, you can use a journal to break through the barriers to find out what is stopping you from fully trusting your intuition. It may be caused by something deep rooted in your past that is still influencing your life now.

Once you've shone a light on the problem, you can then spend time healing through: self-acceptance, forgiveness of others who may have given rise to the problem, and self-love. In my experience, these are the sources of all healing.

When I spoke to Margaret about this she said, "It is very difficult sometimes; you do have these thoughts but don't listen. I try to act on my intuition as much as possible. Usually you miss out on something in life if you don't take notice of your intuition."

Laura said, "Listening to your intuition is paramount if you want to feel happy, content and fulfilled. Whatever choice you have made using it will feel right for you whether or not it is emotionally, financially or socially rewarding. There is no better feeling than doing what you know to be true for you. It is what the term 'gut feel' was invented for after all."

Once you've identified your own feelings that are acting as intuitive signals, you can combine these with the visual clues you learned in Step 2 to communicate more effectively in your meetings with clients. You can use the visual clues to determine whether your words are connecting with the people you are speaking to as these little 'tells' give you an indication of what is going on sub-consciously in the other person.

Use your intuition to pick up on any feelings you have. This can help you to discover whether the relationship would be beneficial to both of you. If it doesn't feel 'right' for you, it may not feel 'right' for the other person. If you go against your gut feeling then the relationship can end up being a non-starter for both parties.

At the same time, your intuition can be giving you signals through feelings you are experiencing as you talk to the person. For example, a person showing visual clues that he or she is disinterested and you may feel a churning feeling, which is making you feel uncomfortable. If the person is interested you experience a warm feeling and know that your words are connecting and you are on the right track.

Try this:

What intuitive feelings do you experience when talking to a person who is?

- Interested in what you have to say.
- Disinterested in what you have to say.

Notes:

Making your intuitive signals stronger

Your body can provide stronger intuitive signals if your mind, body and soul are in alignment. If you feel sluggish because you are fuelling your body with the wrong food stuffs, you won't be so in tune and may misread the signals.

Getting back to organic living, using pure products on your body and avoiding chemicals wherever possible (my pet hate are room plug-ins), drinking filtered water, combined with healthy exercise, can all help your intuitive signals to become stronger.

An effective way to start tuning in more regularly to your intuition is to relax and zone out of today's complications. You can do this simply by going for a walk where you are close to nature, such as in a park, or in the countryside. You can try soaking in a pampering bath with a natural product that contains an essential oil, such as lavender, that will help to quiet your mind and sooth your soul.

You can spend time in more meditative thought whilst walking along the beach or sitting on a park bench. This allows you some quiet time when you can switch off from the hustle and bustle of life and start listening again to your inner voice whilst tuning into the recharging energy of nature.

You can do this when you need some guidance on business decisions you need to take such as setting the right pricing, whether you should work with a particular client, or if you should walk through a particular door that has opened for you. You can also use your intuition when you need to be more inspired in your work.

A great book to help you get back in tune with your whole self is called 'Quantum Wellness A Step-by-Step Guide to Health and Happiness' it was written by Kathy Freston (ISBN: 0091929156).

I realised one day that using my intuition is as natural to me as breathing. It is an involuntary action that is the largest part of my decision making process. I use my intuition to show me that I need to take a particular course if action. If I go against it, or simply don't trust it, the decision I make just doesn't 'feel right'.

In the early days of finding your way with using your intuition you may feel it is wise to keep your thoughts to yourself if you are in the company of people who are sceptical about these ideas. In order to make your intuition grow stronger you need to nurture it and one of the ways you do this is through feeling totally ok about it and talking about it with people who support the same way of thinking. It is totally liberating when you come across people who feel the same way as you even if you don't meet these people and simply read their books to begin with.

What I'm trying to say here is that you can be pleasantly surprised by the people you would dismiss as seeing this as new age nonsense. Protect yourself from naysayers who will put a negative spin on these ideas until you have your own solid proof that it is working for you. Surround yourself with people who support and uplift you with their openness to using intuition in business and have thoughts and ideas on how you can take this further.

Summary

- Your intuitive signals will be distinctive to you and you can do the exercise to find out what they are.

- You can strengthen your intuitive signals by becoming aware of each occurrence.

- Combine your intuitive signals with the visual clues you learned to communicate more effectively.

- Use your intuition to guide your sales decisions, if it doesn't 'feel right' to you - then it probably isn't!

Review

Congratulations! You have now completed the third step of the sales book. Take some time to complete these simple exercises to help you review Intuition:

- Which areas of Step 3 do you feel are causing you the most problems?
- What action do you want to take to overcome these problems?
- What timeframe do you want to give yourself to complete this action?

Notes:

Step 4: Facilitation

Facilitation is all about how you handle the meeting with the client; so that you are both getting the most out of your time together. Start the sales meeting by putting the person at ease by managing their expectations of what you will discuss, how long the meeting will take and how much time they've got (this gives a frame to the meeting).

Reassure them that it's a meeting to get to know each other and it's up to them how they want to take it further (so that they won't feel that they are going to be forced into buying something).

I know it sounds as if you are repeating yourself, but people can only absorb so much information at a time. It will ensure you cover any points they may not have taken in before, and give them a chance to ask you any questions.

For example: You are a life coach holding a taster session with a potential female client (Kay Parsons). You need to frame the meeting by asking Kay how long she's got, or say that the meeting will take about (an hour). This is so that you aren't fighting the clock if she has only thirty minutes until she needs to go and pick up the kids from school and you need sixty.

At the start, thank Kay for booking a taster session with you. Give a brief introduction to what the taster session involves. Reassure her that the coaching session is confidential. Ask her about any prior experience she has had of coaching and what outcomes coaching helped her to achieve.

Use the communication techniques you learned in Step 2 to discover the **problem** she is facing, the **goal** she wishes to attain and the **block** that has been holding her back from achieving it. Once you've asked the questions and listened to her answers; you can tell her about how your products or services will offer the **solution** she is seeking.

Problem	Goal
Kay needs to focus on the problem she wants to solve that led her to agreeing to the meeting with you today. When you start asking her questions she may reveal more than one problem that you can offer the solution for.	Kay needs to imagine her problem solved. To help with this, you can ask her: How will you feel when you have achieved your goal? What will your life be like?
Block	**Solution**
You need to know what has blocked Kay from taking action until now and what could block Kay from taking action in the future. This can include such things as lack of time, money, motivation, or fears that may be holding her back.	Kay needs to know that your products and services can offer the solution she is looking for (at a price she is prepared to pay). You also need to demonstrate to her that you can help her to overcome the block.

Example: Kay Parsons - Life Coaching Taster Session

Problem
Kay has recently taken early retirement at the age of 55 and is getting used to her changed circumstances. She has mixed feelings about retirement. She doesn't know how she is going to fill her time. She has been working full-time for the same company for 30 years. She is divorced. She doesn't currently have a partner and she normally socialises with her work colleagues.

Goal
Kay would like to be fitter and healthier and to lose weight. She feels that this will give her more energy to do things, including going out socially. She'd like to be able to wear the size 12 clothes she has and specifically a red dress that she loves but doesn't fit into at the moment.

Block
Kay lacks motivation; so she put things off to another day.

Solution
Kay would like to join a local gym and take an art class. When you ask her be more specific about losing weight she gives a measurable goal of 10lbs that she'd like to lose within 3 months. She likes the idea of having a life coach to motivate her and keep her on track to attain her goals.

Now you have lots of useful information:

- You know that she has recently retired.
- Her social life was tied up with her work.
- She doesn't have a partner and needs some interests.
- She wants to improve her self-esteem through losing weight and getting fitter.
- She tends to put things off.
- She has specific goals that are measurable.
- She sees the value in hiring a life coach to help her achieve her goals.

Example: Jane Lewis - Web Design Sales Meeting

To show you how this works in practice, in a business to business context, you run a web consultancy and have gained a sales appointment with the Marketing Manager, Jane Lewis, of a small business that is tendering for a new website.

Problem
Jane's boss isn't happy with their current brochure-style website that is looking a bit tired and outdated. Someone in IT built it but they left a while ago. The website hasn't had a makeover for about 4 years.

Goal
Jane would like a new professional looking website. The site needs to attract more clients to the business. She doesn't have any web experience. This is the first big project she has managed and she wants to impress her boss. She needs help to keep the web project on track; so that the site is launched on time. She wants the site to be easy to maintain as she doesn't have much time to spend on updating it.

Block
Jane would need to wait until early in the next financial year to do the work. This will be in about two month's time. Her boss would need to sign it off and the web project also needs board approval.

Solution
Jane needs a web design agency to help her with the redesign. She needs an easy to use content management system. She also needs effective ways to help more potential clients to discover the website.

Now you have lots of useful information:

- You know that she isn't happy with the company's brochure-style website.
- Jane needs help to attract more visitors to the site that convert into clients.
- She doesn't have an existing website designer and the existing website was built in-house.
- She needs a simple hassle-free way to update the site.
- She can't start the work for about two months.

Match products and services

Once you have enough information from your clients to understand the problems they want to solve; you can start matching your products or services that will give them the solutions they need to achieve their goals. Always remember to talk in terms of benefits to them (that relate to their goals) and to weave back into the conversation any personal information that the client has given to you.

If there are any other products and services that you know the client would benefit from, take the opportunity to mention them during this part of the meeting. Think about any other products or services that will add value to the main reason for your discussion e.g. if you are a life coach, you may have informational products such as teleseminars and CDs that your client would find valuable and talk about them now.

Focus on the outcomes

In the life coaching example, you can talk her through the coaching methods you use in the sessions and explain how you will be focusing on the outcomes that she wants to achieve. It is essential to communicate to the client that you have listened and heard what she is saying and that you understand:

- The issues that she is facing.
- The blocks that hold her back.
- The results she is looking for.
- How you can help her to achieve these results.

Tell her about the benefits of your products and services that relate to her unique circumstances. Let her know about other clients you've helped who've benefited from coaching by losing weight, or you helped make the transition and now enjoy being retired, are having more fun, taking up new interests, travelling etc. (obviously within confidentiality boundaries).

Overcome the block

Kay needs to see how the block could stop her from achieving her goal. You can then focus on how you can help her to overcome the block. You may like to ask her how she will feel if she continues procrastinating and doesn't start taking any action. You can also give her some tools that will stop the old pattern before it starts and to catch any negative self-talk, replacing these thoughts with positive new ones.

'I can' and 'I am' affirmations are very effective and using visualisation to experience her life as she really wants it. She can also give herself a reward each time she achieves a task that would make her feel good. Such as having a delicious fruit smoothy instead of reaching for a chocolate bar and acknowledging each time she has done something well. (There is more on Acceptance, Affirmations and Visualisation in Step 5: Reflection). Even if you don't receive the sale you have offered her something valuable that she can use to make a difference in her life.

Reveal who you are

You also want to discover what she would need in order to feel happy to work with you. You can share information about yourself, just as you would in an interview. Open up and tell people about your expertise, your successes and your passion for what you do. People like the personal touch and this normally makes them more receptive to you!

In the web consultancy example:

- You can tell her about how you gained your expertise.
- Jane may want to read testimonials from satisfied clients and view examples of your work.
- She may want you to provide mock-ups of what the new website would look like.
- She may need a proposal to show her boss and other decision makers, such as members of the board.

Talk money

If you have told people when you made contact with them about the price you charge for your products or services, and asked them about their budget, you can overcome any price objection before it happens. If you are asked to negotiate on price, you will need to know beforehand the price you are prepared to do the work for, or say you need to get back to them with a quotation. (There's more on this in Step 5). It is often best to negotiate the price there and then and get a commitment from them at the meeting whilst they are ready to buy from you.

In the life coaching example, Kay should already know what you charge from either your website, or when you made the taster session appointment. However, we all want to know that we are making a good buying decision and so need some form of guarantee that what we buy is going to offer value for money. You can offer people a good deal (e.g. a money saving such as an extra hour for free of your time each month). You can offer people a risk-free trial or a money-back guarantee. You can offer people incentives to buy such as a special offer if they book within a set time.

I recently received a telesales call from a salesperson who was selling a listing in a directory. I was in the middle of doing something, but the sales guy didn't ask if I had time for the call. He talked and talked at me. When he eventually paused to draw breath, I quickly interjected and said that I was busy and didn't have time for the sales call.

I always try to be pleasant as I know how hard telesales is. But he carried on in the same vein. This time I butted in and said that I really didn't have the time. He then changed tact and said that I had to decide there and then so that he could give me a special offer that would be gone tomorrow.

The offer was very good and I would have been tempted to take it. But, his manner was so rude and pushy that I was completely turned off. So I firmly said that I wasn't interested and he slammed the phone down on me!

I wanted to share this to illustrate the other end of the spectrum. How incentives can be used as a way to manipulate and to push people into buying. Either we may have experienced a time when we've been pushed into buying something and then on reflection invariably cancelled, or we know someone who has. What a waste of ours and the salesperson's time. It also doesn't leave us feeling too happy about the company the salesperson works for!

Summarise what you've discussed

At the end of the meeting it is really important to summarise what you have discussed and agreed. Tell her what you plan to do next in terms of follow-up action and agree a timescale for this to be done in. Get permission to contact her again if you need any more information. Ask her if she is happy with everything you discussed and if she has any further questions.

Then leave her to decide whether you offer the best solutions for her. You aren't trying to push or manipulate the person into anything through using 'hard sell' techniques. You are simply offering her options and telling her about what you can do for her that will give the solutions to her problems.

Have faith!

She may not be ready to give you a commitment there and then, she may need to mull over what you've said. Sometimes you have to walk away and just have faith that the sale will complete in your favour! It's tempting to start badgering her if you don't have a lot of work on. Be patient. Give her some time and get on with other sales activities so that you aren't reliant on getting this sale. Release any attachment to the outcome and let it go. You will get the sale if you are meant to.

One cold rainy night many years ago I knocked on the front door of my client's house. As I walked in, his family were sitting around the dining table eating their evening meal. I was ushered into the front room where I sat patiently waiting for him to come and talk with me. Some time later his whole family appeared.

As I sat sipping my cup of tea it became obvious that the appointment hadn't been qualified enough by the telesales person who'd made it for me. There was nothing I could do for him! So I ended up giving him some free advice and then went on my way. About a year later he came into where I was working and asked if he could see me. He'd been given a large sum of money and had remembered me from that night and wanted me to invest it all for him!

Treat your clients respectfully

You obviously need to make sales to earn money. However, this doesn't mean hounding people with endless follow-up calls. Stick to what you have agreed and don't keep ringing them when they haven't made a decision yet. Selling with Heart is all about having respect for your clients. This means delivering on your promises, keeping to deadlines, and letting people make decisions in their own time and own way.

Manage expectations

If she is interested in what you have to offer, she will let you know that she is. If she is happy to buy from you, you then need to manage her expectations of any next steps. Ask for her commitment to complete the activities you agreed during the session. Tell her this will be the key to the results she can achieve from life coaching.

Talk her through the process of what you need to do next and what she will receive for her money. For instance, you could agree on a date and convenient time to deliver a product. If it is coaching, you may need to ask her to complete an exercise before the first coaching session and send this to her via email. Have a diary with you to make the next appointment, or give a timescale in which you'll get a proposal to the client.

Make it clear about your payment terms. If you feel it is right, ask for payment upfront before you start work. If you have to leave documents for signing with potential clients, make it easy for them to return them to you.

Give them a reply-paid envelope, or agree a time when you can pop back to pick them up. It is always best (in my experience) to take any paperwork with you to the meeting. If not, email any documents straight after the meeting with clients when their agreement to the sale is still fresh in their minds!

Once you've made the sale

I remember being told a story about a car salesman. The lady couldn't believe how friendly and attentive he was when he was selling her the car. Soon after she bought the car she tried to contact him because there was a problem with it and she couldn't get hold of him. Every time she rang she was told that he was at lunch, with a client, or not in the building!

This car salesman didn't value his client. He was thinking only of hitting short-term sales targets and not about building long-term client relationships. I learned when I was a sales professional the value of my existing clients who would return again and again for new products. These clients know you, like you and trust you. They are more receptive to buying again from you and generally love to hear from you about any special discounts, or new products and services that become available.

That's why I think women like Selling with Heart as it cares for people. It's about being as good as your word, going the extra mile and taking the time to ensure that clients are still happy after they buy from you.

You may want to consider adding loyalty services to your product offering. These offer your existing clients a good deal. It really frustrates me when companies only offer good deals to new clients and don't reward their loyal existing ones.

You can add your existing clients to your newsletter database to keep your business name in their minds and to continue building a stronger relationship. Contact your existing clients periodically to make sure they are still happy with your products or services. You may like to send a personalised card at the end of the contract period with a special price if they want to renew.

You can also send out customised emails to specific clients. For example, a client who has bought an anti-cellulite cream may be interested in receiving details about body brushes. By doing this you are showing your clients that you remember their individual needs. (Amazon is really good at doing this).

Keep a mental or written note of the personal details that your clients give you, so that you can show that you care by taking an interest in how their vacation went, how their family members are, pets etc. Your clients can see that you view them as people rather than as 'a sale'.

Try this:

- Which of your existing clients would be most receptive to hearing about your new products or services?
- How will you get your existing clients to return to your business to buy more from you? (E.g. Email marketing with an incentive, loyalty discount etc.)
- What InfoProducts could you create that your existing clients would find valuable? E.g. EBooks, CDs, Teleseminars. (Read more about InfoProducts in Step 5: Reflection.)

Notes:

Summary

- Start by putting the person at ease by telling them what you are going to be discussing and how long the meeting will take (this gives a frame to the meeting).

- Reassure the person that it's a meeting to get to know each other and it's up to them how they want to take it further (so that they won't feel that they are going to be forced into buying something).

- You may also find it helps to spend some time at the beginning of the meeting talking about anything other than what you are there for as this can help the person relax.

- Complete any agreed actions promptly and confirm at the meeting that you can go back to the person to ask further questions if you need to.

- Take all the paperwork you need with you such as invoices, contracts or standing order forms so that you can complete the sale there and then or email them straight after the meeting.

- Ask for payment (or a deposit) upfront to help with your cash flow.

- Treat your clients respectfully and take the time to ensure they are still happy after the sale.

Review

Congratulations! You have now completed the fourth step of the sales book. Take some time to complete these simple exercises to help you review Facilitation:

- Which areas of Step 4 do you feel are causing you the most problems?
- What action do you want to take to overcome these problems?
- What timeframe do you want to give yourself to complete this action?

Notes:

Step 5: Reflection

Now we will look at how to learn, improve, and move on, as we all make mistakes in sales. You can use the experience to become more effective. It can be the best feeling in the world when you make a sale and it can be the worst low when you lose one; even though you've put your heart and soul into receiving the business. In my experience, I have found three categories of buyers over the years:

1. **The window shopper**: some people won't buy from you as they are shopping around and intend to go elsewhere.
2. **The worried shopper**: some people will need you to spend more time with them to answer many questions.
3. **The meditative shopper**: some people will need time to think it through before making a buying decision.

Not making a sale is an opportunity to reflect on the experience. What did you do well; what could you have done differently? If you could have done more, make a note of it for next time. Always keep evolving your sales technique by tweaking areas that you aren't happy with until they give you the results that you are looking for.

If you come across a technique used by another salesperson, make a mental or written note of it and incorporate it into your next meeting. Practice makes perfect. It took me about 2 years before I was completely happy with what I was saying in my sales meetings. I kept refining my technique with every person I met until I found what worked best for me. Don't give up, just keep working on it until it becomes second nature to you and you find that more and more people are turning into your clients.

Two selling truths

1. Although we'd love to, we won't receive every sale.
2. Some people aren't destined to be our clients.

In my experience, the sales I don't receive turn out to be a blessing and the people I do attract as clients are the ones I love working with. When I've taken on some work that I wasn't really meant to receive, I've always regretted it. I know in my heart that I'm doing it for the wrong reasons. It often causes a lot of heartache. Looking back at these times, I feel that the money wasn't really worth it.

Negotiating on price

If you can do it without losing face (and you really want the business), then pick up the phone and try to find out the reason why you didn't get the work. If the reason you didn't get the sale is within your control, take any action you can to overcome this problem. Even if you don't receive this sale, you've learned what to do to be more successful next time.

Even though we are working and doing what we love the effort doesn't always equal the reward. So, be really clear in your mind about the real value of what you do and your monetary value to your business.

Don't let people negotiate you down to a price that you can't really afford to do the work for. You are in business to make money! You need to meet your sales targets for your business to thrive and survive. If you can negotiate on price then do it. If you can't afford to, then learn the lesson from the missed sale and walk away!

Getting your pricing right

Running a business often means working in periods of feast and famine. We either have lots of work on and so feel relieved that we can pay our bills or we are scratching around for work. For some reason, there is never a consistent period when we feel that everything is in balance!

We do also tend to undervalue our time and expertise in terms of what we are actually worth. We can give too much of our valuable time to complete the project without getting paid for all the effort we've put into it. I believe the reason for this is that we want to be able to pay our bills and so we will win the sale without a thought for the dent in our self-esteem that comes from undervaluing our time.

What I mean by this, is that if we've taken on a project in this way, our clients are always appreciative and love what we've done for them. However, we feel a sore loser as we've not been paid a fair amount for the work we've put in. We know it isn't our clients' fault, but it sets the tone of the relationship. Repeat clients will then expect us to do work of the same high quality for the same low monetary value.

Your business will suffer if you undervalue your time; you need to be really clear in your mind what you can afford to do work for, whether you are going through a busy time, or a lull. If you set your fees too low, you will find that you haven't got enough hours in the day to earn what you are really worth.

If you create unrealistic expectations at the start of your relationship by giving your clients a lot for their money, it will be harder to start charging them a more realistic amount without damaging the relationship. This is a hard area to get right, but the effort you put in will reap rewards for you and your business in the long run.

If you know you undervalue your time and want to do something about it, if you hate asking people for money, or seem to keep losing out because of price, here are some tools that you can use to overcome these barriers to sales success.

Knowing the minimum amount you can charge

Spend the time working out the minimum amount you can do work for. Let's look at an example of a sales target of £2000 per month. To break this figure down into the minimum amount you need to be charging your clients, you first need to work out how many weeks you work per year. As a sales professional, I set my sales targets based on 44 weeks per year as I would need to allow for holidays, training, team meetings etc.

How many weeks do you work per year?

If you don't work during your children's school holidays, you may work about 39 weeks per year. How many weeks will you work per year? Then you can do the calculations to discover how much you need to earn per working day and per hour. Using the above example this would be:

Example
£2000 x 12 months = £24,000 £24,000 / 39 weeks = £615 per week £615 / 5 working days = £123 per day £123 / 7 working hours = **£17.50 per hour**

Your minimum rate would need to be set at £17.50 per hour for you to achieve the monthly sales target that you require. In the space below work out how many weeks you work per year and how much you need to earn per working day and hour:

Your calculations
• The number of weeks you work per year:
• Your monthly sales target:
• Your annual sales target:
• Divide the annual sales target by the number of working weeks:
• Divide this total by how many days you work per week:
• Divide this total by how many hours you work per day:
• Your minimum hourly rate is:

Feeling undervalued by your clients

According to the Law of Attraction, like attracts like, which means be careful what you think! If you feel undervalued by your clients it may be that you are undervaluing yourself and projecting this out. You may find that your clients are simply mirroring back the thoughts that you are subconsciously giving out. If you want to change this and start attracting new clients who value what you do. Then start to project out that you value yourself. Say this affirmation to yourself daily:

I value what I do

The universe is willing to give you everything that you want in your life. I'm sure you want more of the good things! So try to concentrate on attracting more good things by filtering out the negative thoughts and replacing them with positive ones as they happen.

Using your site to let people know what you charge

A website is a great way to let people know what you charge. Most people interested in what you do will use your website for research purposes. If you are clear about the rates you charge, they are already aware of your fees before they talk to you. It then makes it easier to talk about money as you can refer them to your website, or send them a PDF document of your rates before you meet.

You can also use the website to filter out the 'window shoppers' who are getting quotes and already have the person, or company in mind that they will be using for the work. They are simply shopping around so they can haggle on price and will just waste your time.

Asking clients about the budget they have available

Ask your potential clients what ballpark budget they have available for the project. They won't always tell you as they want to get the best deal possible and so may keep you in the dark about how much they are prepared to spend.

However, if you can find out the budget available it will save you time and energy in the long run. This is because the time spent on a proposal that doesn't result in new business, is time taken from earning money towards your monthly sales goal. You need to be sure that the effort on admin tasks is worth the time not spent in front of clients where you could be earning money.

Knowing the budget available also allows you some breathing space to decide if you want to reduce your rates to get the work. For example, I recently submitted a proposal for an industry that I'd like to work more in. I had a good idea of their budget and so reduced my rates because I know that if I get this project it will lead to further much more lucrative work (and an impressive client for my portfolio).

Making sure you are talking to the right people

In corporate life selling was a numbers game where the more bums you got on seats the more chances you had of making a sale. I don't believe you need to sell like this. You can sell a lot smarter by really clear about who your potential clients are, what they are prepared to pay, and how your products (and expertise) will give them the results they are looking for.

You need to make sure that you are getting in front of the right people who are looking for what you do. Then, once you are face to face (or your website is on their screen) it is down to your sales skills, or how well you have constructed the site, to get the business.

Staying focused on selling

Believe me, it is all too easy to get distracted by the day to day tasks and lose sight of the money making activities! You need to work smarter by taking the time to identify your sales goals. You need to create a document (more on this later) to keep you focused on your targets. You can combine this with some savvy sales ideas that will help you to sell smarter. You can then balance out what you need to do in your day in a way that ensures your business thrives.

Activity is the key to setting and achieving your sales targets consistently. It is all about keeping the momentum going to achieve your sales goals each: day, week, month, quarter and year so that your business continues to grow, whilst giving you the salary you need. It's a disciplined way of working that keeps you focused on your sales goals. It means continuously planning ahead, keeping one eye on the following week whilst trying to achieve your sales targets for the current week.

When you are running your own business, you don't have a sales manager to watch over your sales figures, so it is ultimately down to you how you manage your time to achieve your goals. If you keep sales records you can work out the average sale you receive per client. You can also discover how many clients you needed to see to make one sale.

Keeping sales records

I recommend creating a spreadsheet or word document that you can easily update. I've filled out the one below to illustrate the sort of information that you will need to record each week. I keep a note in my diary and then update this at the end of each week:

Week 20					
Working days	Mon	Tue	Wed	Thu	Fri
Number of appointments made	0	1	2		
Sales made	£0	£350	£150		

Number of appointments made this week	3
Number of appointments made for next week	2
Weekly sales target	£500
Weekly sales achieved	£500
Monthly sales target	£2000
Monthly sales achieved so far	£1000
Yearly sales target	£24,000
Yearly sales achieved so far	£12,000

Allowing for the quiet times

In both my corporate sales and business life I have always had quiet times. The secret is to plan ahead. There will be times during the year that will be quiet such as when people are on holiday and this will obviously depend on the nature of your work. You can compensate for this by: Seeing more people in the weeks leading up to and after this period to make up for the lull in business. Reviewing existing clients to see if they need additional products or services and offering them special offers if they book an appointment soon after the holiday season has ended (say in the New Year).

Keeping all the balls in the air

When you run your own business you have the freedom to control how you do your best work. I see how I feel each day and then choose the work that I want to do that feels right to me. Some things I hate doing (like my accounts), which have a deadline; so I have no choice about when I have to do them! But other tasks on my to-do list can be done any time during the week.

I like to do my Selling with Heart coaching calls on certain days; so that I'm free on other days to choose what feels best for me. One day I'm inspired to write and market my articles, another day I'm inspired to design an advert for the local newspaper. If I try to force myself to do marketing on a day when I'm not feeling in tune with it, I normally end up wasting the day and redoing it much quicker (and better) on a day when it feels right to do it.

We all work differently and women are known for being good at multi-tasking. Look at your schedule. How do you like to work? Would you prefer to see more clients at the beginning of the week? Would you like to have one day a week for admin and one day for marketing? Would you like to do a little bit of everything each day? Would you like to just see how you feel each day and select the task that you are intuitively drawn to?

Don't spend all your time doing what you love!

Running a business means that you often have to do everything yourself. Some days it's hard to pick up the phone to make a sales appointment. It can be put off for another day; so that you can spend your time absorbed in what you love doing.

I know it's easy to put the sales tasks to the back of your mind for the day, which turns into a week and then a month. Suddenly you find that the phone isn't ringing with new orders and you are struggling to pay your bills. In my experience, it pays to set aside some time each week purely for your sales and marketing activities.

Trusting your heart and believing you'll do well

In corporate life I never worried about my sales targets as I always trusted my heart and believed that I'd do well. I trusted that I would achieve what I'd need to each week. I would focus on the day to day sales activities (once I had structured my week using the principles I've shown above). I followed my inner guidance and always did achieve what I needed to. This meant that I wasn't stressed or trying to pressurise people into buying from me to hit my sales goals because I was worried about meeting my targets.

- Do you believe that you can attract what you want into your life?
- Do you worry about money and then suddenly get an enquiry out of the blue?
- Do you get a sense that everything will be alright and that your business will succeed?

Much of this book focuses on the tangible aspects of our work. Trusting your heart in business can take our skills into another dimension. Once you believe you'll do well, you can start to attract the people and business opportunities into your life that you can't even see right now.

A couple of years ago, I had just finished a project and was thinking that I needed a new client. The next morning the phone rang and it was a lady who had been referred by an existing client to me. She became a new client giving me a big order for my business!

Savvy sales idea: Bread and Butter

It is human nature to concentrate on the 'sexy' sales that make big money rather than on the 'bread and butter' that keeps our businesses running. These big sales take up all of our time, keep us on tenterhooks until the very last moment and may take ages to land! Focus instead on the bread and butter sales and the bigger sales will come along as a result of all your activity. In the meantime, you can use these sales to bring in the steady income that will keep your business ticking over.

To give you an example of how this works in practice, I used to sell a product that was only a couple of hundred pounds in commission. It may sound a reasonable amount, but compared to the time I had to spend in paperwork it seemed hardly worth the effort. So, if I saw an opportunity where this product was right for a client, I would recommend it on top of any other products the person was buying. I set myself a target of 100 of these products per year. I worked out that I needed to sell only two to three of these products each week to hit my target. I managed to achieve this target, which gave me nearly £20,000 per annum additional commission!

To give you another example, I mainly work with corporate clients, but they are notoriously slow payers! To bring in some income whilst I'm waiting for the larger invoices to be paid, I will take on work from local small businesses. These projects only take up a couple of days of my time, but I ask for a 100% payment upfront before the work starts. My small business clients pay me promptly as they want me to start the work. I get an injection of money into my cash flow, whilst I'm chasing the larger clients who haven't paid me yet.

Try this:

- List your Bread and Butter products and services.
- How many of these would you like to sell each year?
- Which clients would they be most suitable for?

Notes:

Savvy sales idea: Consider Selling InfoProducts

The sole responsibility for making money rests on your shoulders. Any time you spend away from selling to your clients can have a negative effect on your salary. To help you overcome this, you can consider selling InfoProducts related to what you do.

This means that you can create products to share your expertise with the people who want your knowledge and are prepared to pay for it! This will help you to achieve your sales goals even when you are: asleep, doing your admin, away on holiday, taking care of your kids etc.

When I started out in sales, I was petrified that my clients would know more than me. The truth is that unless they work in the same field as you, you will know a lot more. Even if you do work in the same field, chances are you will have your own experiences and solutions that you have tried and tested.

Remember that you know a lot about what you do and people are prepared to pay for this knowledge. Package what you know and sell it on your website. Write EBooks, run teleseminars and sell CD's of your talks. This is too big a subject to cover here, but if you follow **Savvy Saleswoman** on Twitter, I will let you know of any events that I feel can help you with this:

http://twitter.com/savvysaleswoman

Overcoming fears

You may be held back from sales success by self-limiting beliefs. You can use simple techniques to improve how you feel about yourself and to re-programme your internal tape that's telling you that you won't succeed. You can catch any negative thoughts as they happen and change your behaviour as a result. You can do this by using the following:

- Affirmations
- Acceptance
- Visualisations

Affirmations

You can use affirmations to replace any negative thoughts that you may have locked away into your subconscious over the years. If you think about it, it took a long time to programme them in, and so you need to practice these regularly for your brain to accept them as a more positive reality. The only 'rule' with affirmations is that they need to be in the present tense.

Here are some examples:

- I allow my authenticity to shine.
- I embrace who I am and stand tall.
- I let go of my insecurities.
- I am free to be me.
- I trust my inner voice.
- I let go of fear and trust in the process.

Try this:

- Write down your own affirmations and get into the habit of saying them to yourself regularly.

Notes:

Acceptance

Acceptance means concentrating on the things you do well so that you aren't constantly putting yourself down or letting negative self-talk ruin your self-confidence. You can start to write all the things you like about yourself in your journal to accept what you do well to build your confidence. I've found this is a really powerful way of changing my self-image and repairing my self-esteem.

Keep records in your journal of the things that you accept about yourself; so that you can look back at what you've written to see where you started from to how you feel about yourself now.

Try this:

- List ten things you like about yourself.
- List ten things you have done well today.

Notes:

Visualisations

You can use this powerful tool to train your mind. Visualisation literally means picturing a future event in a way that gives you the best possible outcome. So, for example, you could use it when you have a sales meeting with a potential client that you want to go well. You could use it to visualise a project you have taken on that you are nervous about completing and visualise the project proceeding smoothly and completely successfully.

Relax and close your eyes. Picture the event and then see, feel, smell, taste and hear every single detail in your mind's eye including the people you'll come across reacting positively to your actions. Believe 100% that the event will go well and picture the end result.

I often do this when I have a meeting with a client and want to pick up my cheque at the meeting. I visualise the envelope with my name written on top of it and my client handing me the envelope. So far it's worked when I believe 100% that it will!

You can also use visualisation to alter your current state of mind by revisiting the feeling of being happy, confident, energised etc. You can use visualisation to change your mood; so that you feel that way again. For example, you can visualise feeling relaxed and picture a time when you were before.

Then see, feel, smell, taste and hear every single detail of that time. It could be something as simple as picturing yourself in a warm lavender scented bath. You can be listening to your favourite music. There can be lots of candles giving off a shimmering light. This can help you to feel as calm and relaxed now as you were then.

Try this:

- Visualise a sales meeting going smoothly, the people in the meeting being receptive to you and what you are saying. You look confident and feel calm. You can see them shaking your hand placing the order and the contract being signed. You can even see them handing you the cheque! Spend some time playing around with this visualisation technique picturing whatever feels right to you.

Notes:

Energy

You may already be able to sense energy shifts in the people you come across on a daily basis. You can feel whether people are taking in what you are saying, or are wary, or seem disinterested. Your intuition can tell you when your words are connecting with your clients in business or with the people you come across in your life.

I'm a sensitive soul, which is great as it means that I am very intuitive. I do find negative energy and large crowds of people draining and after these experiences need some quiet time. Through being intuitive you can find yourself taking on other people's energy in a way that makes you feel really out of sorts. I've found that the best way to overcome this is to get calm and centred and let the negative energy leave you by sending out thoughts of love and light.

Gratitude

Each time something good happens say a simple THANK YOU! You may like to write down 10 things everyday that you are grateful for having in your life. I make a point of always saying thank you mentally when I have received a blessing in my life, such as a new client that I love working with. Gratitude acknowledges the gift and opens you up to receiving even more – in addition to being good manners!

Summary

- Some people aren't destined to be your clients
- Not receiving a sale is an opportunity to reflect on the experience. What did you do well? What could you have done differently?
- If you can negotiate on price then do it. If you can't afford to, learn the lesson and walk away.
- Keep focused on your sales activities – don't just spend all your time doing what you love!
- Use affirmations, acceptance and visualisations to overcome self-limiting beliefs in sales.

Review

Congratulations! You have now completed the fifth step of the sales book. Take some time to complete these simple exercises to help you review Reflection:

- Which areas of Step 5 do you feel are causing you the most problems?
- What action do you want to take to overcome these problems?
- What timeframe do you want to give yourself to complete this action?

Notes:

Last thoughts

This book introduced you to listening to your inner voice and letting it guide you to making wise choices. Selling with Heart means speaking from the heart, talking honestly about what you can do for people, being yourself and delivering what you say you will. These are the reasons that people will buy from you. Not because you've used a hard sell technique to talk them into it. In my experience this means happy clients, referrals and being able to sleep well at night!

I sometimes walk away from a sales meeting feeling totally drained but know that I have given my clients my full concentration. We all have off days, and times, when we aren't fully listening and are distracted by our own thoughts. I've discovered that Selling with Heart works best if you give your clients 100% of your focus.

Now it's up to you to: Trust your inner voice. Hear its guidance. Follow your heart. Be free to be you. Be true to yourself. Be kind to yourself. Don't let others stand in your way. Let go of fear. Trust in the process. Embrace who you are and stand tall. Be bold. Best of all be you!

Thank you! I'd love to hear from you

I am truly grateful that you were guided to this book. Please do give me your thoughts about it and send me any success stories. You can contact me via email at: **julie@savvysaleswoman.co.uk** I also have a website at: **www.savvysaleswoman.co.uk**

Lightning Source UK Ltd.
Milton Keynes UK
24 June 2010

156013UK00001B/69/P